Me and Sal Paradise

✓✓✓

Charles Rammelkamp

FUTURECYCLE PRESS
www.futurecycle.org

This book is dedicated to the memory of my twin brother,
Robert Rammelkamp, 1952–2016.

Published by FutureCycle Press
Athens, Georgia, USA

ISBN 978-1-942371-62-5

Contents

Part One: Prologue

Part Two: Hitchhiking 1971

Part Three: Hitchhiking 1972

Part Four: Hitchhiking 1973

Part Five: Coda

Part One: Prologue

Hitch Hike

I'm packin' up my bags,
I'm gonna leave this town right away.
Hitch hike (hitch hike, baby)....
I loved that song
on the Stones' 1965 album,
Out of Our Heads, the hit
song of which was "Satisfaction."
A cover, written by Marvin Gaye.
I was just thirteen,
hadn't heard of Jack Kerouac yet,
Sal Paradise or Dean Moriarty;
just starting to deal
with pimples and masturbation.

Chicago City,
that's what the sign on the freeway read.
Hitch hike,
Hitch hike, baby.

"Should we stop and give that guy a ride?"
I asked my mom
as we eased onto the highway entrance ramp,
headed from Potawatomi Rapids
to an appointment in Muskegon.

The man with his thumb out,
wearing jeans and sneakers,
appeared to be in his twenties,
a small suitcase by his leg.

"Are you kidding?" Mom exclaimed.
"Never, *ever,* pick up a stranger."

Hitch hike.
Hitch hike baby.
Hitch hike.
Hitch hike, children...

Runaway

"We struggled hard all our lives to get by."
—Lennon/McCartney, "She's Leaving Home"

The day my twin brother Bob ran away,
fled to California without informing
our parents of his plans,
he swore me to secrecy.

We walked together
to the middle of town,
a bright Saturday in early June.
Shoppers thronged Main Street
in those days before
they abandoned it for the strip malls
near the highway entrances
where my brother was headed.

We shook hands
for the first time in our lives,
like a rite of adulthood,
then parted company,
but only after he promised
he'd call our parents
within the next few days.
He seemed either unaware
or simply didn't care
they'd be frantic with worry.

If Bob had stayed behind,
our parents would have made him go to college
or take a job in the steel factory.
No other options in Potawatomi Rapids, 1970.

So he had to get out
the only way he could,
and I had to keep his plans confidential
until finally that evening
when my mother called us to dinner.
I let them know what I knew,
the knowledge that had made
my head throb all that afternoon,
the knowledge that broke their hearts.

Part Two: Hitchhiking 1971

Gimme Shelter

"I'm eighteen and I don't know what I want."
—Alice Cooper, "I'm Eighteen"

Fridays spring semester I was free
after my World Lit class ended at ten:
a dog off its leash, out of my cage.
I'd never really hitchhiked for distance before,
but I decided I'd thumb my way
down to Saint Louis,
a hundred miles south, to see
Gimme Shelter, the movie about
the Stones' disastrous Altamont concert
where the Hell's Angels murdered a kid.
A huge Rolling Stones fan,
I was sure the movie would never
come to Nibana; no way
I'd see it in Potawatomi Rapids, either.
Besides, it would be an adventure.
Isn't that what I wanted?

Hitching down was an easy A,
Basketweaving 101 for football jocks:
a man and his son picked me up
almost as soon as I stuck out my thumb,
just a few blocks from campus,
drove me all the way to the Tivoli Theater
on Delmar Boulevard. Beginner's luck.

But getting back? Not so easy.
Nobody stopped for me in rush hour Saint Louis,
Friday evening, everyone with plans,
cars whizzing past, horns honking.

A couple of cops in a patrol car
took me to the Poplar Street Bridge
near the Arch, let me out with a warning,
but at least I was no longer their problem.

I hiked across the Mississippi
on the thin strip of sidewalk, a fugitive
feeling the heat and suction of passing cars.
Short rides in Illinois, mostly walking,
as the sun sank out of sight.

Finally, close to midnight, in Roodhouse,
a local patrolman pulled me over,
ordered me into the cruiser;
scared, sure he'd arrest me, fine me, jail me,
I struck a punk's defiant pose,
but instead we just waited for a passing truck driver
headed up 67 through the dark.
The officer asked him to let me out in Nibana.
I wish now I'd been more grateful.

A couple of weeks later,
Gimme Shelter showed up at the State,
the art deco movie palace in the town square.
My friend Jack, pals with the owner,
scored free tickets for about a dozen of us.

Part Three: Hitchhiking 1972

Zen Koan

"Have you ever been to Toronto?"
Almost rhetorical, Moira's question
introduced her Canadian winter observations
but also provoked a memory from my youth.
A Canadian herself,
Moira described the severe winters, the cold,
Toronto's pedestrian tunnel system,
but all I could think of was hitchhiking
from Michigan to Montreal the summer of 1972
with my college friend Mark.

In London, Ontario, we'd gone to a pub—
the drinking age only 18 and we were 20,
still illegal in the Midwestern states.
We joined a couple of girls at a table,
drank some beers, tried making conversation
over the jukebox music and loud voices.
After a time, the girls, feeling free,
kissed us with open mouths
before they left our table.

Drunk, aroused, no place to go to sleep,
not having thought this through,
we decided to keep on hitching,
though it was pitch dark
and we were still 450 miles from Montreal;
Mark's sister had an apartment near McGill.

By chance a sports journalist,
on his way to an assignment, picked us up:
He was going to Montreal too!
All three of us crowded into the front seat,
the back packed like an attic
with luggage and equipment.

The next thing I knew
I was blinking my eyes open in Quebec,
an awful taste of hangover in my mouth.

"You slept right through Toronto!" Mark laughed.
"Your head kept falling on Todd's shoulder,
saliva drooling from your mouth."

"No, not really," I demurred,
though Moira hadn't expected an answer.

I remember the Taoist riddle,
Chuang Tzu dreaming he was a butterfly,
then waking up to wonder if maybe
he was really a butterfly
dreaming he was Chuang Tzu.

Lay Across My Big Brass Bed

Mark and I hitched down from Montreal
through a torrential rainstorm off the Saint Lawrence River,
continuing all the way past Lake Champlain,
drenched like river rats,
clothing pasted to our bodies.

We intended to visit our friend Fred in Hempstead,
but right around Saugerties we realized
we were perilously short on cash,
and we felt defeated anyway,
the weather lashing us like galley slaves.

So we decided to head back to the Midwest,
thumbed east along 212 through Woodstock—
three years after the music festival.

A bearded young man with hair to his shoulders
driving a pickup truck loaded with antiques,
teetering like an unbalanced barge in a canal,
picked us up outside Bearsville.
The weather had cleared; our luck changed.

Almost the first words out of his mouth:
"You guys want to get high?"
We drove to a secluded hilltop
where he fired up his pipe.

Somehow Ben started talking
about the antiques business.
"Ever since Dylan sang that song,
all anybody wants is a brass bed,"
he laughed, looking at the chairs
and chests-of-drawers in the truck bed
as if at a bunch of unwanted orphans.

Ben only took us as far as Phoenicia,
but it seemed as if we drove on forever,
Lay Lady Lay looping through my looped brain,
the wind-driven ride down from Canada
now just a distant memory.
Might have been a hundred years ago.

Song Sung Blue

If Mark hadn't made a pass at Shirley,
the large-breasted hippie chick
in the psychedelic Volkswagen van
that stopped for us near Oneonta,
we might have had a ride
all the way to Ann Arbor.

Loyal, engaging, funny, irreverent,
Mark nevertheless had inflated notions
about his magnetism to the opposite sex,
an Adonis of the skin magazines;
liked to tell stories of erotic conquests
to widen the eyes of our college classmates,
though part of me, skeptical,
always whispered, "bullshit."
Maybe why we got along so well—
he could see I wasn't hoodwinked.

So we barely get to Binghampton
when from the back seat
Mark, hypnotized by Shirley's patchouli,
rests his hand on the passenger headrest,
snakes it down her bare tanned arm,
as if to cup her breast.
Don't do it! my mind screams
as if watching an innocent child
entering a dark room, in a horror film.

The driver, Billy, whom I'd assumed
was Shirley's boyfriend,
abruptly pulls over
near the SUNY campus,
orders us out of the car.
But then he has second thoughts.

"You," he says to me,
"you can still come with us to Ann Arbor.
I think I can trust you
not to feel up my sister."

I won't lie I wasn't tempted,
but I stuck with my buddy.

11

On the Road

"No, we're just here to see the Falls,"
I told the Canadian official
at the pedestrian border booth.
Mark and I looked a mess,
unwashed, unshaven hoboes
crossing from the USA,
our plan to cut across Ontario to Michigan.

A car full of teenage girls—
all three in the front seat—
had picked us up in Buffalo,
newly minted drivers
on a Saturday afternoon adventure
in their parents' car.

We tried living up to the role
they'd thrust upon us—
romantic carefree hippies,
thumbing gaily across the country—
not too tough for Mark
with his long red hair and beard.
Flirtatious without being threatening,
we cajoled them into taking us
the extra twenty miles to Niagara Falls.

We thanked them when they let us out,
but they were just as grateful
for the story they'd tell their friends.

"OK," the uniformed guard said grudgingly,
suspicion an occupational hazard,
the long line of people behind us
making it simpler to just pass us on.

So we walked into Canada,
gawked at the magnificent falls,
then found ourselves
at the Queen Elizabeth Way entrance headed west.
We'd make Port Huron by sundown,
but still I thought longingly of those Buffalo girls,
how I'd like to go with them to that imagined party.

Bridge Over Troubled Water

"Get out! The fucking thing's gonna blow!"
Dale slammed his shoulder
into the driver's side door
and dove to the pavement,
a paratrooper bailing out of an airplane.
Mark and I tumbled out the back doors,
hoping the Rambler behind us
would stop in time.

A small fire burned under the chassis
of Dale's station wagon.
He'd sensed the flames somehow,
maybe felt the heat,
while we drove over the Blue Water Bridge
from Point Edward to Port Huron,
the Saint Clair flowing below.

August in Ontario, the sun still hung
like an orange coal in the sky
after eight in the evening.

Dale'd picked us up outside Sarnia,
just when we'd about given up
on crossing into the States before dark.

Now we hung on the guardrail, not sure
what country we were in,
while Dale sprayed some sort of dry chemical
under the car.

"You guys better beat it," Dale ordered,
his voice an echo from under the car,
"before the cops get here..."

"Sure you don't need any help?"
I asked, hoping he'd say no.

"Beat it," he repeated.
"It'll just mean more explaining
if they find you here."

America

Russ and Ramona broke off from the pack,
circled back like lone wolves on their Harleys
to where Mark and I stood by the road,
early morning just south of Flint
where we'd spent the night under a tree,
automobile plants thudding in the background
like something out of Fritz Lang.

"Where you guys going?"
Russ yelled above the roar of the bikes,
a sailor at sea in the midst of a typhoon.

"Potawatomi Rapids," I shouted back,
"other side of the state."

"We're headed for the Straits,
but we can take you as far as Saginaw."

The two looked like they'd just rolled around
in a stew of Sunday comic strips,
tattoos up and down their arms,
a wallpaper of symbols, words, images,
silver daggers, crosses dangling from earlobes.

Mark hopped on behind Ramona,
throwing his arms around the inner tube
that was her spreading belly.
I got on behind Russ, more secure
but still jealous of Mark.

"OK, let's go!" Russ shouted,
leader-of-the-pack fashion.

An hour later they dropped us at an exit
and took off north with their crew.

"It took me four days to hitchhike from Saginaw,"
Mark mused in a sing-song.

"I was just thinking the same thing.
We've come to look for America."

Hippies

"You all ain't hippies, is you?"
The sweet stench of tooth decay wafted through the gaps
of the man's jack-o-lantern smile
as he stared out at us
through the rolled-down window.

Mark's hair curled at the neck,
his red beard a bird's nest,
but mostly we looked like dirty hoboes:
unwashed, unshaven for a week,
clothing—jeans, T-shirts—wrinkled and limp.

"Nah, just trying to get to Potawatomi Rapids,"
I replied, aiming for an *aw-shucks* tone.
"Going anywhere near there?"

"I can take you kids far as Newaygo,"
the man speculated. "Long's you pay for gas."
He looked down on his luck.
"Just don't want no hippie peace freaks.
I was in 'Nam. It ain't been easy."

"We aren't hippies," I affirmed,
giving Mark the eye, knowing
that was how he thought of himself,
Neil Young in his mind.

How I wished I'd said *ain't*
as we swung into the backseat
of the beat-up Chevy,
watched the pavement slide by
through the missing floorboard.

Reputation

The Ford Maverick pulled up beside us
somewhere between Coopersville and Fruitport.

"Hey, 'zat you, Gladstone?
The hell you doing way out here?"
I recognized the floppy Dumbo ears,
the pointy rat face of Kevin Broxholm.
He looked us up and down,
taking in the dirty clothes, the duffel bags.
"Need a lift back to Potawat?"

Grateful, Mark and I climbed into the back seat.
The cherry farmer who'd picked us up near Grand Rapids
had let us out in the middle of nowhere,
as if playing a malicious joke on us.
We'd been trudging for miles.

"What are you doing out here?" Kevin asked.
He'd been a couple years ahead of me in school,
now a local in Potawatomi Rapids.
I'd heard he worked in one of the steel factories.
He'd always been into cars,
coveting first one muscle car and then another.

"Been to Montreal. Just getting back."

"I thought you'd be back in college by now."
His voice dripped scorn for schoolboys.

"Next week."

"Who's your boyfriend?"

"This is Mark Matthews,
a college friend from Chicago."

"We always wondered why
you never went out with girls,"
Kevin's rat face scrunched into a smirk.

I rolled my eyes at Mark.
So this is how they peg you at home.
I didn't say anything,
Kevin suddenly fiddling with the radio,
covering his embarrassment.

"Where's Bob at? Still in Frisco?"
He meant my twin brother,
who'd fled Potawatomi Rapids
a couple of years earlier,
on the strength of his thumb and will,
like an escaped convict
making a jailbreak.

"I heard he was living with Phyllis."
Kevin tried to make it sound casual,
but he'd always had a major crush on her.
So had I.

So Long, Yellow Brick Road

I'd spent the summer in Potawatomi Rapids,
earning money for the fall,
on a crew painting the dormitory rooms
at the local college.
The dorms were going co-ed that fall.
Their semester had already started.
The trip to Montreal was my summer vacation.
Mark was a chum from the dorms at Nibana,
a would-be rock musician
I'd met when we both went out
for the spring semester's college play,
Rosencrantz and Guildenstern are Dead.

After we'd washed up and eaten
and talked about our trip with my parents
(so *relieved* we'd made it back safely;
I felt guilty remembering their anxiety
the year Bob ran away to California),
Mark and I walked downtown,
Main Street a destination for local kids.
Those old enough went to Charlie's,
a local watering hole, for beers and pizza.

"Hey! Look!" I cried, pointing
at a new time-and-temperature display
hanging over the sidewalk
outside the First National Bank.
"Times Square comes to Potawatomi Rapids."

Mark, a city boy, looked at me, amused.

I blushed. "It wasn't there when we left."

Next day Mark took off for Chicago.

"See you next week at college," I promised
as we shook hands
by the highway ramp headed south.

But Mark didn't go back to school that fall.
Determined to make it as a rock star,
he sought his future elsewhere.
Last I heard, he was working
in a record store in Athens, Georgia.
Or was it a Western Auto in Indianapolis?

Part Four: Hitchhiking 1973

The Highway That's the Best

After a summer slipping
long-players into sleeves
at a Capitol Records plant in Nibana,
I told my parents
I planned to visit Bob.

Overjoyed but suspicious,
my father wanted to know
how I was going to get there,
all the way to the end of the country
from the middle of the Midwest.

Anxious about my twin brother,
they totally backed my intention:
I wasn't spying or telling tales,
but I'd let him know how Bob was doing.

"I thought I'd hitchhike," I announced,
trying to keep the *asking-for-permission*
out of my voice,
a factory laborer, after all,
living in an apartment of my own,
an adult who made his own choices.

"Well, OK," my father
granted permission nevertheless.
I was still his son;
he was still paying my tuition—and my rent.

My heart leapt anyway,
Jacob stealing Isaac's blessing.
I hadn't even thought how I'd get there.
Route 66?
It winds from Chicago to L.A....
I'd need to check a roadmap.

Five'll Get You Ten

"Five'll get you ten
that trucker's been up all night
popping little white pills."
Red lifted his right-hand index finger
from the steering wheel, pointing at the semi-truck
barreling past us on I-80. *Bull's eye!*
The little Ford Pinto shimmied in its wake,
me in the back with my duffel bag.

Eyes still on the road, Red spoke to me
out of the side of his mouth,
Gloria, sitting shotgun, her hand on his thigh,
smiling as if at the slickest-talking
late-night talk-show host.

I, too, liked being included
in Red's wise-guy confidences.
They weren't married, I could tell,
when Red said something like,
"Five'll get you ten your old man's
already sloshed on six martinis at his club,"
right after they'd stopped for me near Galesburg.

When they dropped me outside Des Moines,
I half-wished they'd include me
wherever it was they were going.

Sensing my ambivalence, Red assured me,
"Don't worry, buddy! Five'll get you ten
the next ride takes you all the way to Frisco!"

Dear Prudence

The college boy on his way to Sioux Falls
dropped me at a service station
on I-80, just north of Omaha,
a good ride halfway across Iowa.
His backseat filled with books and clothing,
he said he needed the company
to stay awake. We talked sports.

But the next guy, a sweating salesman
with a clip-on tie
who picked me up on the exit ramp headed west,
told he'd take me as far as Lincoln,
about an hour down the road,
only he'd have to borrow a few bucks
for gas once we got there.
But he swore he'd pay me back.

He seemed to be a loner, around forty,
hair in a thinning blond pompadour.
I'd just turned twenty-one in June,
now headed for San Francisco
to visit my twin brother
before college started again in Illinois.
He only grunted when I tried to talk,
hands pasted to the steering wheel,
sweat glistening like jewels
on the dark hairs of his fingers.

At a service station
on the interstate outside Lincoln,
he insisted he'd pay me back,
but we'd have to go to his place in the city.

"Sure," I agreed, but while the service jockey filled the tank,
about thirty-five cents a gallon,
I had second thoughts.
"Forget it," I waved. "On me. Thanks for the ride."

"But I can pay you back," he swore,
and I knew then I was taking my bag
and getting out of the car.

The next ride took me all the way west.

Flowers in Their Hair

"All the way to San Francisco?"
the spidery little guy in shorts and T-shirt remarked
as I settled into the passenger seat.
"When I saw you just had that little bag,
I figured you were going only a few miles
down the road, Denver tops."
His disappointment was like an accusation.

"My brother lives out there,
I'm going to see him before
school starts again," I explained,
as if apologizing for being caught in an outrageous lie,
and I wondered about Julian's apparent resentment,
as if he'd made a huge miscalculation
he was certain to regret.
Was it paranoia, imagining the thought bubble
hanging like a halo over his head?: *Oh shit!*

"Name's Julian," he said, offering his hand.
I would have said, "Same as my father,"
except he pronounced it, *Who-lee-yan.*

What a stroke of good fortune I'd felt
when the Peugeot slowed and stopped
on that long stretch of pavement to the interstate—
like a gangplank leading to a mysterious pier—
after I'd left the sweating salesman in his Impala
at the gas pump outside Lincoln.
A life rope thrown overboard.

"OK, but I'll need you to help pay for the gas,"
Julian conceded, resigned,
checking traffic, then swinging onto the interstate.

"No problem!" I promised.
Such a strange vibration.
People in motion.

The Hayseed

"Spent the summer in Ann Arbor
with a woman. It didn't work out"—
Julian's laconic explanation
why he was driving west
at the end of August.

Besides, he taught Spanish at Berkeley,
lived in a commune on Telegraph Avenue.
"Mainly I'm all about being politically engaged,"
Julian clarified, full-disclosure style.
"The Case-Church Amendment says no more bombing
in Southeast Asia, but even Schlesinger admitted
to over 5,000 secret bomb raids in Cambodia
the last few years.
You can't trust that bastard Nixon
to obey the law."

I didn't know what to say
beyond a grunt of agreement,
not very political myself but
certainly on his side.
My secret ambition when I got to San Francisco?
Though I knew I wouldn't do it,
I dreamed of joining a Zen monastery.
Either that or score with a hippie chick.

Julian seemed annoyed by my response.
"So you're from Illinois, huh?
Like, in the middle of a cornfield?"
He had me pegged as the quintessential hayseed,
a blade of grass between my teeth—
the cartoon hick figure I'd be for him
for the next three days, until he dropped me off
at a cable car stop on Market Street.

Hear Me Roar

Helen Reddy's anthem of the summer
spilled out of the radio like triumph itself,
Julian tapping along on the steering wheel
while I sank into my private thoughts.
Haven't seen Bob in almost two years.

Suddenly we swerved to the side of the road.
Two guys with serious travel gear
stood with thumbs out by an exit
near the western end of Nebraska.

"Need a ride?"

"Yah!" one of the boys cried in a German accent,
unburdening himself of his pack,
a turtle shedding its carapace.
They slung their stuff into the trunk,
climbed behind us into the backseat.
I knew that optimistic feeling of relief
coming off them in waves like X-rays.

"We are going to Denver," Mats told us,
as if reading from a phrase book.
Students from Osnabrück, Mats and Niels
were backpacking across the United States.

"OK, I can take you
as far as Cheyenne," Julian told them,
"then you'll take 25 south."

"Yah," Mats agreed.

"Great. I need a break
from this fascist from the cornfields,
going all the way out to San Francisco."
Julian looked my way.
I laughed at his joke.

Cheyenne Showdown

"You're as bad as the fascist bastards," Julian accused.
"It's people like you
who let them get away with murder."

"What did I do? I didn't do anything."

"Exactly. You didn't do anything."

"Well, there's no more draft, at least,"
I pointed out, "not since January."

"So you saved your ass, huh?
All that matters.
You and your corn crop, nothing else."

"Hey, I used to do draft counseling."

"Did you?" The doubt amounted to accusation.

"Kind of, yeah," I fudged,
though it hadn't been since high school.
But was it any of Julian's business?

We sat over sandwiches in a Cheyenne saloon.
It felt like high noon, a gunfight building,
and I sure didn't want to lose my ride
this far from San Francisco.

"I'm all about peace and love, Julian,"
I joked, self-effacing.

Julian laughed,
the tension gone
like smoke in a dream.

"You're six years late, my friend."

"If you're goin' to San Francisco," I crooned,
"be sure to wear some flowers in your hair."

"Way too late," Julian muttered.
We clinked glasses.

Sinbad and the Great Salt Lake

Outside Salt Lake City,
Julian stopped for the two German boys
we'd picked up in North Platte
who'd left us in Cheyenne,
enormous packs on their backs,
like the old man riding Sinbad
in the *Arabian Nights* tale.

It felt like a reunion,
a million-in-one coincidence,
coming upon them by the side of the road.

"Oh, the police stopped us," Mats blurted,
excited as a kid telling his parents
about a celebrity's visit at school.

"But we pretended not to speak English,"
Niels laughed.
"They finally left us alone."

"What did they want to know?"
Julian seemed suspicious of sinister motives.

"What did they want to know?" Niels consulted Mats.
They both tried to remember.
"Oh, you know, where we are going,"
he shrugged, "where we are from."
"It was too much trouble for them!"
Niels and Mats laughed at the memory.

Julian raised his fist in the air.
A blow against the fascist state.
Me? I just thought it was funny,
like Sinbad tricking the old man
into getting drunk on wine,
losing his vise-like grip on Sinbad,
the captive escaping his fate.

Twins

"There is a town in north Ontario,
With dream comfort memory to spare."
—Neil Young, "Helpless"

When they needed to discuss private matters,
Mats and Niels spoke German,
though sometimes with a clandestine air,
as if even being overheard meant compromise.
Their exclusive bubble in the vastness of America.

Like twins, I thought, remembering how Bob and I
had our own private language
growing up in Potawatomi Rapids,
references that down through the years
would become private shorthand for emotions,
situations, personalities, memories.
Our little town and all it signified,
a bedrock even years later when we buried
our father, our older brother, our mother,
captured in the confidential code
of a secret language.

"We'll stop in Elko for the night," Julian announced.
He'd made this trip several times before.
We'd get to San Francisco
sometime the next afternoon.
"Find a cheap motel
where we can crash for the night."

We'd been on the road all day from Cheyenne,
stopped to frolic by the Bonneville Salt Flats
about an hour or two down the road
from where we'd picked Mats and Niels up again—
Julian's treat for our foreign friends,
a taste of the American West,
though it was new to me, too.

Mats and Niels huddled in the back,
conferring in German, weighing their options,
until finally Mats agreed,
"Yah! Yah, we stop in Elko."

28

The Soft Landing

When I got to my brother's apartment
on Clayton Street, in the Haight,
welcomed by him and his girlfriend,
I still felt overwhelmed by my journey,
too soon to let it go,
even though Julian's handshake
had the finality of a closed door,
knowing we'd never see each other again.

After our night in a fleabag motel
in Elko, Nevada, two to a double-bed,
the Germans on one, Julian and I on the other,
we drove uneventfully through the desert,
stopped for lunch in lovely Reno,
and then on into California,
skirting Sacramento, a matador dodging a bull,
making it to San Francisco by late afternoon.

On one level Julian wanted me to know
I was nothing to him,
even an ideological adversary;
on the other, I sensed grudging acknowledgement
of our three-day companionship in his handshake.
Then the three of them drove away,
and I boarded the cable car.

"How was your trip?" Bob and Phyllis asked.

Did I feel like Odysseus coming home to Ithaca?
Well, three or four days on the road
wasn't exactly ten years at sea
after ten years of war.
No need to aim for the grandiose.

"Okay," I shrugged.

Bob and Jack

My brother was a great Kerouac fan;
the Beats in general—
Cassady, Ginsberg, Burroughs, Herbert Huncke
and all the rest—
but Kerouac was his literary idol.
He read and re-read all the novels—
On the Road, The Dharma Bums, Big Sur,
Desolation Angels, Mexico City Blues, Doctor Sax—
identified with the Kerouac characters,
Sal Paradise, Raymond Smith;
read all the biographies and memoirs
by ex-wives, girlfriends, Beatnik
hangers-on, devout disciples.
In love with the myth
of Kerouac's spontaneity, he embraced
the hedonistic road trips across America.

Bob spent months on the road
in the west, the southwest,
until he finally settled in San Francisco
where he'd originally gone
when he left Potawatomi Rapids,
a homing pigeon coming to roost in Haight-Ashbury.

After he and Phyllis broke up,
Bob headed south through Mexico,
into Central America, where
he met his wife in Tegucigalpa,
lived for years in Mazatlán,
crisscrossed Mexico, living by his wits.
What had been an adventure for me
was more of a lifestyle for my brother.

Eventually Bob and Lourdes settled in LA,
but still he planned elaborate trips—
Tahiti, Turkey, Tunisia—
always in the spirit of Kerouac
shipping out in the merchant marines.

Cancer finally caught up with Bob.
Now Lourdes is taking his ashes
back home to Honduras.

Part Five: Coda

Good Clean Fun

We was just having some fun
on a Friday night after work,
must have been nineteen sixty-eight, sixty-nine.
We was working construction, the five of us,
had a few beers after work,
just driving around Des Moines
looking for something to do,
when we seen this long-haired hippie
standing by the side of East Fourteenth,
thumb stuck out for a ride somewhere.
Said he was going to a meeting in Iowa City.

We told him we was going that way,
threw him in the back of the pickup,
drove out to a farm near Winterset,
where we give him a beer
then shaved his head!
Man, we left nothin' but peach fuzz!

But it was just good clean fun.
Nobody got hurt or nothin'.
We give him a dollar,
took him out to the highway,
then drove on into Winterset for more beers.

But the hippie'd got our license,
reported us to the sheriff, old Jim Rouse,
who tracked us down at a Winterset tavern,
charged us with assault.
We was fined fifteen dollars apiece
plus four dollars court costs.
But you know what?
I'd do it all over again
if I had the chance.

Now that Trump's the president,
maybe folks won't be so sensitive, so *touchy.*
I just wish I was still young enough
to have me some more good clean fun.

Acknowledgments

The Five Two: "On the Road"
Tipton Poetry Journal: "Flowers in Their Hair"
Meat for Tea: "Runaway," "Twins," "Cheyenne Showdown,"
    "Song Sung Blue," "Zen Koan"
Plainsongs: "Hippies" (winner of *Plainsongs* poetry award)

*Cover artwork by Gene McCormick; author photo
by Roman Gladstone; cover and interior book design by
Diane Kistner; Chalkboard text and titling*

About FutureCycle Press

FutureCycle Press is dedicated to publishing lasting English-language poetry books, chapbooks, and anthologies in both print-on-demand and Kindle ebook formats. Founded in 2007 by independent editor/publishers and partners Diane Kistner and Robert S. King, the press incorporated as a nonprofit in 2012. A number of our editors are distinguished poets and writers in their own right, and we have been actively involved in the small press movement going back to the early seventies.

The FutureCycle Poetry Book Prize and honorarium is awarded annually for the best full-length volume of poetry we publish in a calendar year. Introduced in 2013, our Good Works projects are anthologies devoted to issues of universal significance, with all proceeds donated to a related worthy cause. Our Selected Poems series highlights contemporary poets with a substantial body of work to their credit; with this series we strive to resurrect work that has had limited distribution and is now out of print.

We are dedicated to giving all of the authors we publish the care their work deserves, making our catalog of titles the most diverse and distinguished it can be, and paying forward any earnings to fund more great books.

We've learned a few things about independent publishing over the years. We've also evolved a unique, resilient publishing model that allows us to focus mainly on vetting and preserving for posterity poetry collections of exceptional quality without becoming overwhelmed with bookkeeping and mailing, fundraising activities, or taxing editorial and production "bubbles." To find out more, come see us at www.futurecycle.org.

www.ingramcontent.com/pod-product-compliance
Lightning Source LLC
Chambersburg PA
CBHW060046050426
42448CB00012B/3132